Natural Disasters

Furious
Floods

Julie Richards

Chelsea House Publishers
1974 Sproul Road, Suite 400
Broomall, PA 19008-0914

The Chelsea House world wide web address is www.chelseahouse.com

Library of Congress Cataloging-in-Publication Data Applied for.

ISBN 0-7910-6580-4

First published in 2001 by
Macmillan Education Australia Pty Ltd
627 Chapel Street, South Yarra, Australia 3141

Copyright © Julie Richards 2001

Edited by Sally Woollett
Text design by Polar Design Pty Ltd
Cover design by Polar Design Pty Ltd
Illustrations and maps by Pat Kermode, Purple Rabbit Productions
Printed in Hong Kong

Acknowledgements
The author and the publisher are grateful to the following for permission to reproduce copyright material:

Cover photograph: Hurricane Hugo storm surge hitting Puerto Rico, courtesy of Australian Picture Library/CORBIS.

AAP/Barry Skipsey, p. 4; AP/AAP, pp. 2, 3, 7 (bottom), 29, 31, 32; Australian Picture Library, p. 18; Australian Picture Library/Andrew Gregory, p. 26; Australian Picture Library/CORBIS, pp. 6, 7 (top), 8, 14, 22–23 (all), 24; Australian Picture Library/Fritz Prenzel, p. 21; Australian Picture Library/ J. Carnemolla, p. 5; Bureau of Meteorology, pp. 12 (bottom), 25; CSIRO, p. 12 (top); National Oceanic and Atmospheric Administration/Department of Commerce, p. 17; PhotoEssentials, p. 20; PhotoDisc, p. 19; Planet Earth Pictures, p. 11; Reuters, pp. 10, 27, 28.

While every care has been taken to trace and acknowledge copyright the publishers tender their apologies for any accidental infringement where copyright has proved untraceable. Where the attempt has been unsuccessful, the publisher welcomes information that would redress the situation.

Contents

The power of water

Collecting shells and interesting pebbles from the sea is fun.

What if you found these shells and pebbles in your backyard—and your backyard is a long way inland or on a very high hill?

Do you know what it means?
It means that many thousands or millions of years ago the **sea** was there!

Water can change the landscape **quickly**, **dramatically** and **forever**.

Entire towns can be **swept** off the map and cliffs sent **tumbling** into the sea.

Water can behave like an enormous battering ram, **drowning** areas in minutes and **tossing** huge objects as if they were toys.

WATER is one of the most important things on the planet. The Earth cannot survive without it. Yet, for many people, water can be the cause of all their problems. What happens if it keeps on raining? Can we stop a flood? What starts a **tsunami**? Water is a very powerful force of nature.

Not all floods are bad, but when they hurt or kill people and destroy property they are called natural disasters.

What is a flood?

Most of the Earth's surface is covered in water. The banks of rivers and lakes and the beaches and cliffs stop the water from spreading over the land. Sometimes, these natural barriers are not enough to keep the water where it belongs. When water flows over dry land it is called a flood.

Floods cause widespread **devastation**.

Land can flood very quickly after heavy rainfall from a sudden thunderstorm. Other floods can happen in places where there has been no rain. Sometimes the cause of the flooding is a long way away. When this happens, people are surprised by the raging water that rushes towards them, destroying everything in its path.

Human-made floods

Not all floods are caused by nature. Some crops need a lot of water to grow, so farmers flood their land each year by digging trenches from the nearest river to their fields. As water flows down the river bed, some of it runs into the trenches. The trenches carry the water to the crops. This is called **irrigation**.

Sometimes a concrete wall called a dam is built across a river. The dam stops the river from flowing. Because the water cannot go anywhere, it builds up behind the dam and spills onto the surrounding land, making a lake. This lake is called a reservoir. Water is collected and stored in **reservoirs**. It can then be piped into towns and cities for drinking water, pumped to farms to irrigate crops, or used to make a type of electricity called **hydro-electric power**.

Dams are one way of controlling rivers and preventing floods. However, a dam can burst because of the incredible weight of the water behind it.

Where do floods happen?

Floods can happen just about anywhere—even in the desert. In June 1991, a freak storm brought snow and rain to a desert in Chile, South America. It turned one of the driest places on Earth into a flood plain.

Flood plains and deltas

Flat, low-lying places that are close to the sea or a large river system are often in danger of serious flooding. Rivers carry rich soil that is excellent for growing crops.

When a river floods, it spreads this soil over a wide area. As the water drains away, farmers can plant their crops and look forward to a good harvest. A flat area around a river that floods when the river is full is called a **flood plain**. A flat area between two or more rivers is a **delta**.

Bangladesh is one of the poorest countries in the world. It sits on a low-lying delta close to the coast and between two of the world's largest river systems—the Ganges and the Brahmaputra. Bangladesh is often devastated by great storms that push the sea over the shore or when the rivers carry too much water. Thousands of people are drowned or swept away. Their villages disappear in seconds.

Many islands in Indonesia rely on floods to bring rich soil to their farmland. If this did not happen, they would struggle to feed their populations.

The Turag and Buriganga rivers overflowed onto the low-lying land in Bangladesh in September, 1998.

Disaster Detective

Rain gauges were used in India as long ago as 400 BC. Farmers would place a number of bowls in different places to catch rain. This helped them to learn about the patterns of rainfall. You can do the same and make a chart or graph to show what happened.

When do floods happen?

Floods happen when there is too much water in one place and it cannot escape quickly enough. What do you notice about water when you spill it?

➤ Water always spreads out and flows downhill.

➤ Water will drain away or soak into some things but not others.

Most flooding happens when there is too much rain and it cannot be drained quickly enough. However, snow and ice, earthquakes and volcanoes and even wind can cause floods to occur.

Swirling hurricane Hugo had one of the worst **storm surges** on record.

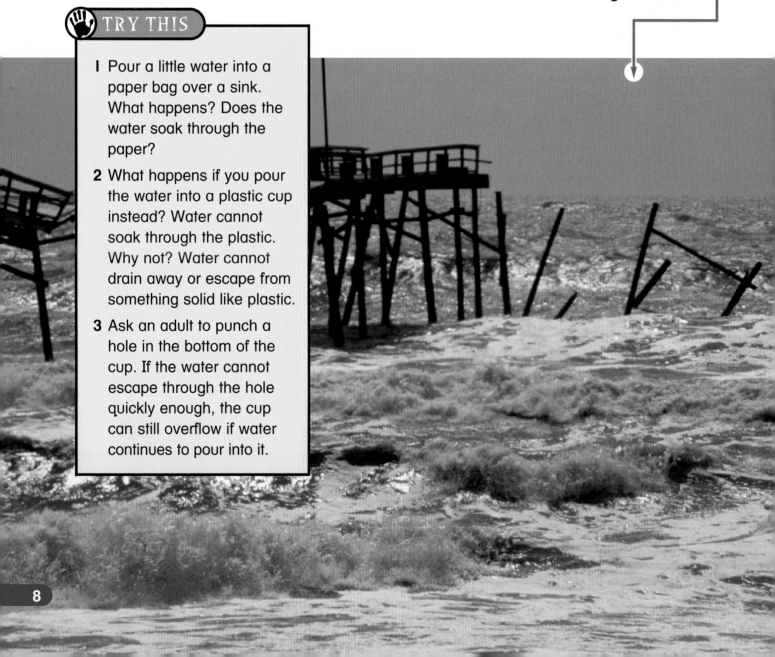

TRY THIS

1 Pour a little water into a paper bag over a sink. What happens? Does the water soak through the paper?

2 What happens if you pour the water into a plastic cup instead? Water cannot soak through the plastic. Why not? Water cannot drain away or escape from something solid like plastic.

3 Ask an adult to punch a hole in the bottom of the cup. If the water cannot escape through the hole quickly enough, the cup can still overflow if water continues to pour into it.

Rainfall and flooding

There are many ways flooding can occur. A flood that happens very quickly is called a **flash flood**.

Thunderstorms

Rain from a thunderstorm falls fast and heavily. All this extra water can find its way into a river. If the river cannot move the water away fast enough, it will reach the top of the river banks and run onto surrounding land.

A lake is like a bathtub with the plug in. Leave the tap running and what happens? There is only one way the water can escape—over the side of the bathtub. Just like the bathtub, the lake will keep on rising until it overflows, unless the rain stops.

Water that is not held in by river banks or dam walls is soon out of control because the water spreads out and follows the slope of the ground.

GUESS WHAT?

For over three billion years the Earth has been using the *same* water. It is simply reused through the water cycle.

Where does all the water go?

GUESS WHAT?

Each raindrop in a storm grows around a speck of dust so small that you cannot see it. The amount of water in an average thunderstorm weighs about the same as 25 cars.

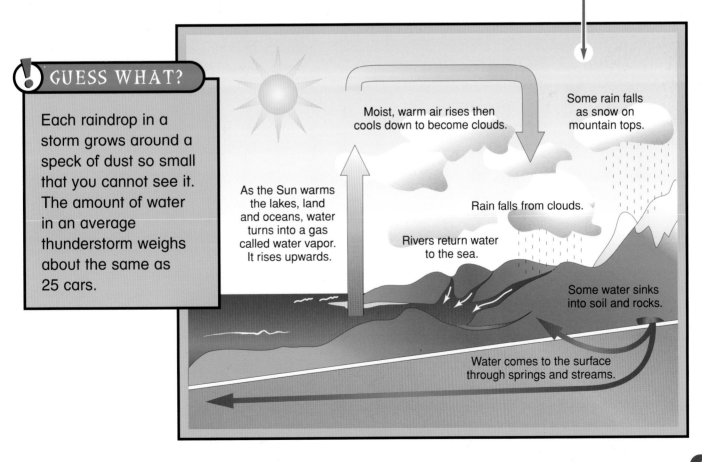

Moist, warm air rises then cools down to become clouds.

As the Sun warms the lakes, land and oceans, water turns into a gas called water vapor. It rises upwards.

Some rain falls as snow on mountain tops.

Rain falls from clouds.

Rivers return water to the sea.

Some water sinks into soil and rocks.

Water comes to the surface through springs and streams.

Even though everyone knows a monsoon will bring almost constant heavy rain, it still makes life difficult.

Monsoons

You may have heard people speak about a **wet season** or a **monsoon**. Monsoons are winds that change direction at certain times of the year. When they do, they bring very wet weather. In some countries the monsoon or wet season divides the year into two parts: a wet season and a dry season. During the wet season, people expect heavy rain to fall almost constantly.

If the wet season starts early, or goes on for longer than usual, the land becomes so full of water that no more rain soaks in. Instead, the water runs along the top of the ground. It can also wash soil into nearby rivers and lakes, clogging them up. Slowly, the rivers and lakes will fill to overflowing.

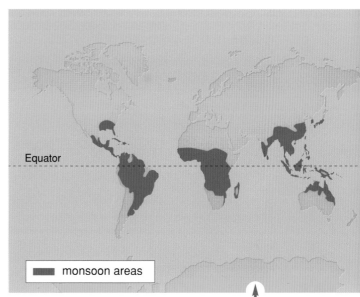

Equator

 monsoon areas

What do you notice about the areas of the world that experience monsoons? They are very close to the **Equator**.

Snow and ice

In some countries, snow and ice cover high mountains for most of the winter. The snow and ice begin to melt when warm spring weather arrives. Most of this water flows down the mountain in mountain streams.

If heavy rain falls at the same time as 'the melt' begins, there will be much more water than usual rushing down the mountain slopes. The streams and rivers will run fast and deep. That makes them very dangerous.

El Niño

Water and air constantly circle the Earth. The direction in which water or air flows is called a **current**. Ocean currents follow the winds that cover large parts of the world. If one of these winds does not blow as strongly as usual, warm currents in the Pacific Ocean push their way into the colder water near the coast of South America. The fishermen who live in the South American country of Peru have called this warming of the ocean **El Niño** (pronounced *el neen yoh*).

When ocean waters become warmer, more water rises into the atmosphere, creating more rain than usual in that part of the world. At the same time, this change can cause other parts of the world waiting for rainfall to stay dry. In 1983, when El Niño warmed the ocean for longer than usual, the world's weather changed a lot. Terrible floods happened in North, South and Central America, while severe drought in southeastern Australia resulted in a more **intense** wildfire season.

These swirls in the ocean are made by moving currents.

Disaster Detective

Oceans cover more than two-thirds of the Earth. The Pacific Ocean is the largest ocean and covers nearly one-third of the planet. It contains more water than all the world's seas and oceans put together. If you put all this water into one place, you would need a square tank 886 kilometers (551 miles) long.

You might like to find out about other bodies of water. See if you can find out where the largest lake, sea or dam is. See if you can collect some interesting facts about water.

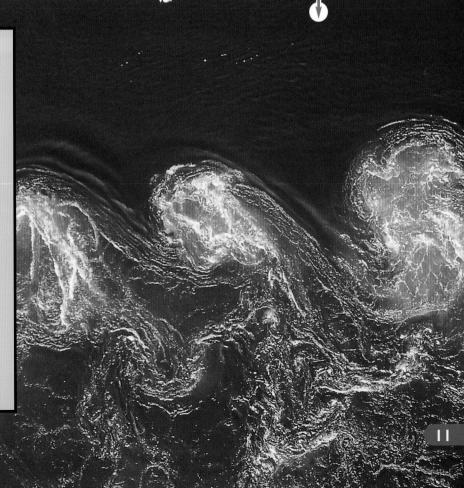

How can a drought cause a flood?

A drought happens when little or no rain has fallen for a long time.

During a drought the top layer of soil on the ground dries out. This means that plants growing in the soil die because they cannot get the food they need to grow. When the soil becomes extremely dry a **dust bowl** develops. Because there are no longer any plants to hold the soil together, high winds pick up the dust and blow it hundreds of kilometers away.

Droughts can continue for years. As the ground dries out, it becomes harder. When the rain finally comes, the hard ground is like a solid barrier and the water sits on top of it. This can cause major flooding.

During a drought the ground becomes so hard and dry it cracks.

During one drought in Australia in 1983, 200,000 tons of soil was lifted from the ground by strong winds. It floated in a great cloud across the city of Melbourne.

Flooding from the sea

Sea floods

Great storms that develop over the sea have fast winds that whip up waves and drive them in towards the shore. While many coastal towns have sea walls to protect them, sometimes they are not strong enough to withstand the weight of the water. The constant pounding of the waves weakens them until they collapse.

Storm surge

Severe storms called tropical cyclones sometimes form over the sea. As the cyclones move across the oceans, they lift the sea into an enormous wave and push it ahead of them. When this wave reaches the coast it crashes onto the beach and floods sweep everything away. This is called a storm surge.

The storm that follows this wave brings with it rain so heavy that it almost falls in solid sheets. Severe flooding is always a problem.

GUESS WHAT?

Some tropical cyclones are so big they can actually fill the whole of the sky over a small country such as Bangladesh. A tropical cyclone can contain billions of tons of water. In some parts of the world, farmers rely on these storms to provide enough water for crops to grow and prevent famine.

Flood waters caused by a storm surge have drained away, leaving this boat stranded.

What else can cause a flood?

Global warming

The Earth is getting warmer. Already, some of the ice near the North and South poles is beginning to melt. When glaciers melt they add more water to the ocean, making it higher.

You can see this for yourself when you next have a drink. Fill a glass halfway to the top with liquid and add some ice cubes. When the ice melts, do you notice how close to the top of the glass the liquid goes? The same thing happens with the sea. As it gets higher, low-lying land becomes flooded.

The Maldives islands off the coast of India are made of coral reefs. As oceans rise higher, these low-lying islands are being worn away by the waves.

Read All About It!

Ice Sheet Causes Continents to Sink

Some parts of Europe and northern America are still feeling the effects of the last Ice Age that happened 18,000 years ago. The heavy ice sheet that once covered these continents began to disappear. Without the ice pressing down on it, the land gradually rose, getting back its old shape.

Today, some of it is still rising. This makes other parts of the land tilt downward into the sea.

Volcanoes and earthquakes

The power of an erupting volcano is so great that it can shake the ground around it. This shaking can loosen soil and rocks. If enough rocks slide into a river, they will act like a dam and the water will build up behind them. The water will have nowhere to go but over the banks and onto the land around it.

Like a volcano, an earthquake can cause soil and rocks to slip down into rivers and dams, or even crack a dam wall. The weight of the water resting against the wall can weaken it enough to make the dam burst.

Sometimes when an earthquake happens or a volcano erupts beneath the sea it can cause the most powerful, awesome and deadliest wave in the world—the tsunami.

What is a tsunami?

A tsunami is a long, fast and extremely powerful wave. Often, it is more than just one wave. Several waves may arrive one after the other. Earthquakes, volcanoes and landslides that happen near or under the sea can start a tsunami.

A tsunami is different from an ordinary wave. Ordinary waves are made:

➤ by the wind blowing across the surface of the water

➤ by the movement of the sea coming in and going out again. This movement is called a **tide**. Tides happen because the Sun and the Moon keep pulling on the Earth like a magnet

➤ when the tide has to squeeze into a very narrow river. When a massive amount of water is funnelled into a tight space in this way, it can pile up into an immense wave that surges up the river. This is called a **tidal bore**.

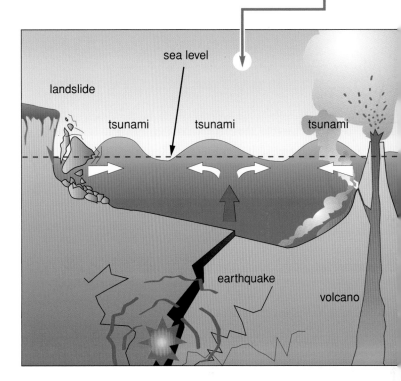

When earthquakes, landslides or volcanoes rock the ocean floor, they can start a tsunami.

sea level

landslide

tsunami   tsunami   tsunami

earthquake

volcano

Where do tsunamis happen?

Tsunamis always begin in the ocean, but the death and destruction they cause never happen until the waves crash onto the land. Tsunamis have visited every coastline at one time or another. However, they happen more often in the Pacific Ocean. Why? This is because the Pacific Ocean has more volcanoes and earthquakes than anywhere else has.

Read All About It!

Volcano Blows Island in Two

When the volcanic island of Krakatoa, near Java, exploded in 1883, it was so violent the island was split in two. So much water surged from the ocean depths that tsunamis circled the Earth for days afterwards.

How does a tsunami form?

When an earthquake shakes the ground beneath the ocean, the ocean floor rises and bends before dropping back down again. A sudden, jerky movement like this pushes the water upwards. The water **churns**, forming strong waves.

In 1896, a strong earthquake shook the bottom of the sea near Japan. Nobody really noticed it because it was hardly felt on land. Twenty minutes later, the ocean began pulling back from the beaches into waves and fish could be seen flapping about on the ocean floor! When the tsunami hit, one of the waves rose higher than a ten-story building! About 27,000 people were drowned, and 10,000 homes washed away.

These pictures show a car park before, during and after a tsunami in Japan.

How does a tsunami travel?

Each wave in a tsunami may be up to 320 kilometers (200 miles) apart. The deeper the water, the faster the tsunami will go. They can move faster than a jet aircraft and travel across the ocean in less than a day!

In deep water, tsunami waves are very small, so small that they cannot be seen from an aircraft or felt by sailors on a boat. It is only when the tsunami nears the coast that the waves rear up to reach terrifying heights.

What makes a tsunami so high?

Shallow water near the beach acts like a brake. As the tsunami slows down, the water begins to pile up and curl into a gigantic wave. In seconds a wave that is only small becomes enormous just before it breaks across the beach. If more waves arrive they can all jam together, pushing the tsunami even higher.

GUESS WHAT?

After an earthquake in Chile, tsunamis spread out in all directions and travelled as far as New Zealand and Japan. Even though they had travelled a great distance, the waves were still six meters (20 feet) high when they struck the coast.

These enormous waves struck the Japanese coast as the result of a tsunami.

GUESS WHAT?

All the oceans of the world are extremely deep. Along the bottom, huge mountains with steep valleys and winding canyons can be seen. The deepest known canyon is found in the Pacific Ocean. It is called the Marianas Trench. Even Mount Everest would disappear without a trace if it were dropped into the Marianas Trench.

What can happen during a flood?

Rushing water can travel faster than a car. The weight of a large amount of water that is moving at great speed can knock houses and bridges over and carry them away as if they were toys! No matter how good a swimmer you are you will be no match for the raging waters of a flood.

Flood waters are dark and thick with mud. It is almost impossible to see dangerous objects that can cut, tangle or knock a person unconscious. Drowning is the greatest cause of death during floods because some people think they can walk, swim or drive through the water.

If you can see a tsunami on the beach it is far too late to escape. Nobody can outrun a tsunami. People who try to rescue others after the first wave has hit the beach are often swept away by the next waves.

Read All About It!

Oil Tanker Sails Down Main Street

When the Brisbane River in Queensland, Australia broke its banks in January, 1974, a huge oil tanker was ripped from its moorings. The *Robert E Miller* floated crazily down the main street, almost crashing into a block of flats, before two tugboats were able to stop it.

Drowning is a great cause of death during floods because people do not understand the power and force of rushing water.

Forecasting and measuring floods

A **meteorologist** is a weather scientist. One of the most important jobs a meteorologist does is to warn people about severe weather and the problems it may cause. By collecting information about rainfall, meteorologists try to work out where and when flooding may occur. This is called making a forecast. Meteorologists also keep a check on river heights, sea tides and whether or not snow is melting on nearby mountain tops.

All of the world's weather happens in the Earth's atmosphere. Meteorologists depend on technology to help them find out what is happening in the atmosphere and how it might affect the weather.

Tsunami warnings

A network of stations monitors earthquake and volcanic activity around the world. Another network has the important job of measuring the height of the tide in different places. These networks send the information they collect to the Pacific Tsunami Warning Center in Hawaii. The scientists there can use the information to locate tsunamis and warn people who are threatened by these waves.

When an earthquake or volcano large enough to trigger a tsunami is recorded, everyone goes on alert. Information is sent to the Tsunami Warning Center by satellite.

Technology helps meteorologists collect information about what is happening in the atmosphere and to forecast how weather may be affected.

Equipment

Satellites

Meteorologists collect information about the weather from **satellites**. Satellites are small spacecraft that travel around the Earth, watching the atmosphere from space. They can measure the temperature of different parts of the world and send back pictures of cloud formations or track the paths of storms. Knowing where large storms are forming is very helpful when forecasting floods.

Radiosondes

A **radiosonde** is a special balloon with a package of weather measuring instruments attached to it. It floats up into the atmosphere and measures temperature and moisture. When it reaches a certain height the balloon bursts and the radiosonde falls back to Earth. Twice each day, meteorologists around the world release radiosondes so that they can be as up to date as possible on what is happening high up in the clouds.

The first weather satellite was launched in 1960. Satellites have made weather forecasting easier and more reliable.

Can floods be prevented?

Flooding is something that some of us might see during our lives. You may already be living in an area where flooding happens regularly. Perhaps you can find out what kind of preventative measures are taken to avoid disaster.

Different countries have different ways of preventing flooding.

Dikes

The Netherlands is a country in Europe. Much of the Netherlands is very low-lying and constantly threatened by flood. To help prevent floods, a system of **dikes** was built. Dikes are walls made of stone, earth and sand. As long as the water does not rise too high and run over the dikes, flooding is prevented. In 1953, during the North Sea flood, the dikes were not able to stop 1,800 people from drowning in their homes.

In the Netherlands, dikes are used to prevent flooding.

GUESS WHAT?

The Yellow River in China is known as 'China's Sorrow' because in over 3,500 years it has killed millions of people. In 1887, nearly two million people died. In 1931, flooding killed over three million and in 1938, the death toll from a flood was 900,000. Many people died because the floods caused massive landslides.

Levees

A **levee** is a wall made of earth or sand that runs along a river bank. Some levees occur naturally when soil builds up into ridges along the side of a river. Levees can also be made by people. Along the Mississippi River in the United States of America (USA), levees are so wide that roads have been built on top of them. The whole system of levees on this river is longer than the Great Wall of China.

In countries such as India, temporary levees are quickly built when floods threaten small villages during the monsoon. These levees are usually made of sandbags.

Sea walls and groynes

Beaches protect the mainland from flooding by absorbing the force and energy of the ocean's waves. The action of the tide coming in and going out constantly drags sand and pebbles out to sea. Some of the beach will be dragged further down the coast. The special name for this is **longshore drift**. Longshore drift can slowly wash the beach away.

Barriers built of concrete, wood or metal help stop or slow longshore drift. These barriers stretch from the beach into the water and are called sea walls or **groynes**.

The Thames flood barrier has ten gigantic steel gates. These can be raised and spun around to form a wall that stops the sea from surging up into the city of London.

Groynes must be checked and maintained so that they can stand up to the constant pounding of waves.

Flood gates

In England, the Thames River flows through London and out into the North Sea. In the past, severe storms have driven the sea up the river and right into the heart of the city. To make it worse, the city of London is so heavy that it is sinking. Each year, the chance of a flood becomes greater. To solve the problem, a flood barrier was built across the river.

The barrier has ten steel gates that can be raised to block the river and stop the sea from flowing upstream and into the city.

Natural flood prevention

Sand dunes

When the tide goes out, the wind dries the sand on the beach. Dry sand is then blown further up the beach where it piles up into hills. These hills are called sand dunes. Plants that have deep roots, like marram grass, grow very well in the sand dunes of beaches. The roots keep the sand in its place and prevent the dunes from being blown away.

Unfortunately, if a beach is used often enough, these grasses become trampled and lots of feet can wear a track through the dunes. When the wind blows through this track it can destroy the dunes, leaving the land or the cliffs with little protection from the sea.

The bottom of the cliff where this house sits has been slowly eaten away by the sea. When rain soaked into the soil, the house became too heavy and it collapsed.

GUESS WHAT?

Terrible floods in central Asia nearly 2,000 years ago caused many people to leave their homes and seek shelter in nearby lands. The refugees brought new arts and crafts to the peoples of southern China, Korea and Japan, greatly enriching their culture.

Plants and trees

Plants and trees are nature's own defence against flooding. They help to prevent flooding in three ways.

➤ The roots of plants hold the soil together and prevent it from being washed or blown away.

➤ Plants use a lot of rain water for growth.

➤ Branches and leaves on the forest floor slow rain water down.

Perhaps the biggest change taking place on Earth at the moment is the clearing of the world's forests. If the plants are not there, the soil will be washed away and rivers will flood more easily if heavy rain falls.

The world's population is growing very fast. More and more forests are being cleared to make room to grow food. Without trees, more water flows into rivers and lakes. The risk of flood becomes greater.

Protection from floods

It is not always possible to prevent floods. Sometimes, all that can be done is to warn people that a flood will happen. If there is enough time, as many people as possible may be moved to the safety of higher ground. This is called evacuation.

If a flood is coming, everyone needs to stock up on canned food, bottled water, flashlights, batteries and transistor radios. Those living on higher ground may not need to be evacuated, but they may still find themselves cut off by flood waters for several days.

Flood warnings are made available in as many ways as possible.

Flood warnings

If a flood seems likely to happen, meteorologists will issue a flood warning. Flood warnings and river heights are broadcast on radio and television, posted on the internet, recorded on telephone information services and supplied to all the organizations that will be needed to cope with emergency.

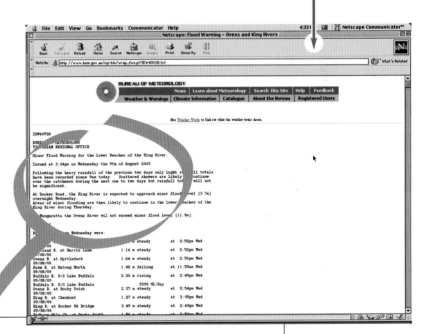

```
IDW40V28

BUREAU OF METEOROLOGY
VICTORIAN REGIONAL OFFICE

Minor Flood Warning for the Lower Reaches of the King River.

Issued at 3:04pm on Wednesday the 9th of August 2000

Following the heavy rainfall of the previous two days only light rainfall totals have
been recorded since 9am today. Scattered showers are likely to continue over the
catchment during the next one to two days but rainfall totals will not be significant.

At Docker Road, the King River is expected to approach minor flood level (3.7m)
overnight Wednesday.
Areas of minor flooding are then likely to continue in the lower reaches of the
King River during Thursday.
```

A gauge that measures water levels can warn people that a flood might happen.

How high will the water go?

If you have ever driven through the country, you might remember seeing something that looked a little like a giant ruler sticking out of the ground near a river, road or an area of low-lying land. This is a called a **gauge**. If the area around the gauge floods, the measurements show how high the flood waters are.

Floods are classified like this:

➤ Minor flooding: some roads may be closed and some low-lying land may be covered by water.

➤ Moderate flooding: larger areas of land will be covered by water, and farm animals will need to be moved to higher ground. Some houses will be evacuated; some major roads and bridges may be closed.

➤ Major flooding: very large areas of land will be under water. Towns and cities will be cut off, and roads and railways will be closed. Many people will need to be evacuated, and power supplies and communications may be disrupted.

After a flood

Safety and disease control

One of the first jobs to be done after a flood is to turn off the power supply. Electricity is very dangerous because it flows easily through water and is invisible. This will happen if power lines fall into the water, or if the flood flows over electrical equipment that is still turned on. Many flood victims have been killed by electricity in this way.

It is important to get food and fresh water to the survivors as quickly as possible. Although they might be surrounded by water, it is extremely dangerous to drink. Flood water may contain mud, rubbish, dead bodies and animal **carcasses**. It can also fill up sewers and drains to bursting point. If filthy waste water and all the other rubbish carried by the flood gets mixed up with fresh drinking water, disease will soon break out.

 Read All About It!

Floods Wash Away Land Mines

After 18 years of war, the countryside in Mozambique is littered with land mines. Some of the land mines have been removed. However, the floods of March, 2000 carried away nearly two million land mines and nobody knew where they went. Parts of Mozambique were without electricity for a long time after the floods because repairers were afraid of stepping on land mines.

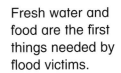
Fresh water and food are the first things needed by flood victims.

Rescue and shelter

Shelters will be set up after a flood so that everyone has a safe place to sleep. Those that have been injured will get medical help. Some people may need to be rescued from their rooftops.

In the African country of Mozambique, the storms that caused the floods in March, 2000 continued to bring **torrential** rain and high winds for several days afterwards. This made it too difficult for the helicopters to fly in and rescue people or drop supplies. Many people had little choice but to drink the filthy water as they waited for days on their rooftops. One woman even gave birth to a baby while still clinging to the branches of a tree!

Helicopters can rescue people stranded on rooftops. They can also drop vital supplies if roads and bridges have been washed away.

Disaster Detective

Amazing Cockatoo Rescue!
During the floods of 1974 in Brisbane, Australia, the Coles family suddenly realized that they had left their pet cockatoo behind in their flooded home. Paul Coles paddled one-and-a-half kilometers (nearly a mile) back to the house on his surfboard and floated in through an open window. He was just in time—there was only a tiny space left at the top of the cockatoo's cage. Putting the cage on a tire, Paul pushed it to safety. See if you can find other flood stories about amazing pet rescues.

Cleaning up

Anything left standing after a flood will be coated in thick layers of mud. Rubbish will have been washed inside buildings. All of this must be cleaned up thoroughly. Some of it will never be properly clean again. Cranes and bulldozers are used to clear away collapsed buildings and wrecked vehicles. Some buildings may have been washed away by the fierce speed of the water and will need to be rebuilt. Special collections of money, food, blankets and other essential items will be organized by aid agencies such as the Red Cross and the Salvation Army. A lot of help is needed to get everything back to normal.

Animal carcasses and dead bodies must be collected immediately to prevent the spread of disease. The water that is still lying in pools or puddles will soon become stale and begin to smell. Mosquitoes can breed very quickly in this water. They can spread serious diseases like malaria when they bite people.

The future

Crops covered by water will rot and die. If there has been a sea flood, the salt water can ruin the soil. It may be a long time before crops can be grown there again. People whose lives depend on the production of food need special help when floods devastate their land. Floods have started many famines.

Countries in the developing world are especially at risk. They rely on richer countries to help them avoid famine and rebuild their lives.

This village in Korea has almost been destroyed by flooding.

Record-breaking floods

The worst floods in recent history

China

In the last 2,000 years there have been more than 1,000 bad floods along the Yangtze River.

The fastest flowing flood

Italy

In 1966, flood waters tore through the city of Florence at 130 kilometers (80 miles) per hour.

The highest ever rainfall in 24 hours

La Reunion

In 1952, a tropical cyclone dumped 1.87 meters (six feet, two inches) of rain in one day on this tiny island in the Indian Ocean.

The highest tsunami

Japan

In 1771, a tsunami caused by an earthquake under the sea, which hit Ishigaki Island, was estimated to be 85 meters (278 feet) high—about the same height as a 25-story building.

The wettest place on Earth

Hawaii

Rain falls on Mount Wai'ale'ale in Hawaii for 350 days of the year. The average rainfall in a year is about 12,346 millimeters (486 inches). That is enough to cover six adults standing on each other's shoulders.

Glossary

carcass	The body of a dead animal.
churn	Stir up and tumble about violently.
current	The direction in which air or water flows.
delta	A flat area of very fertile land between the mouths of two or more rivers.
devastation	Severe damage or destruction.\
dike	A wall of earth, sand and stone built to keep out the sea and stop flooding.
dust bowl	An area of land where the soil has become so dry it has turned to dust.
El Niño	A change in ocean temperatures that affects the world's climate.
Equator	An imaginary line around the middle of the Earth.
flash flood	A flood that happens very quickly.
flood plain	Flat land beside a river that often floods.
gauge	A measuring instrument.
groyne	A barrier built to stop the beach being dragged further down the coast.
hydro-electric power	Electricity made from the energy of moving water.
intense	Extremely hot.
irrigation	Watering crops by altering the path of water from a river using trenches.
levee	Earth banks along the side of a river.
longshore drift	The movement of sand and pebbles along the coastline.
meteorologist	A weather scientist.
monsoon	Winds that blow from the sea, bringing almost constant heavy rain for part of the year.
radiosonde	A package of weather instruments used to measure weather conditions in the upper atmosphere.
reservoir	A place where water is collected and stored for later use.
satellite	A spacecraft that sends back information about the weather to Earth.
storm surge	When a tropical cyclone lifts the sea into big waves and pushes them towards the shore.
tidal bore	A wave created when a large amount of water is squeezed into the narrow opening of a river.
tide	The movement of the sea coming in and going out again from the beach.
torrential	When a huge amount of rain pours down very quickly.
tsunami	An enormous and powerful wave caused by the ocean floor moving during an undersea earthquake, landslide or volcanic eruption.
wet season	A time of year when the monsoon wind brings heavy rain.

Index